THE POOL CUE BOOK

A Buying Guide

By Stephen Mayhew

Merrimack Publishing, Inc.
Bradford, MA

Mayhew, Stephen

The Pool Cue Book
1. Sport 2. Billiards 3. Pool (Game)

Published by:

Merrimack Publishing, Inc.
717 South Main Street
Bradford, MA 01835

978-469-9311
978-469-9316 (Fax)

First Edition
Library of Congress Catalog Card Number: 97-074025
ISBN: 0-9660794-0-X
Printed in the United States of America

1 2 3 4 5 6 7 8 9 10

Book and Cover Design by Gail Stratos
Pool Cue Illustration by Adrian Desrosiers
Cover Illustration by Lisa Plumley

Dedication

To Paul, as promised, and to Ray, by surprise.

Acknowledgments

The author would like to thank Mark Kulungian and the following people for their contributions to this book: Robert Byrne; April Evearitt; Richard Chudy (Richard Chudy Custom Cues); Paul Drexler (pfd Custom Cues); Joel Hercek (Hercek Fine Billiard Cues); Bob Jewett; Jack Koehler; Will McCaffrey; Bill Newsted; Paul Rubino (Rubino Cues); Ray Schuler and Ivan Lee (The Schuler Cue); Regie Simino (Westmoreland Specialty Woods); Patricia Spangler (A.E. Schmidt Billiards); and Tim White. A special thanks to my able editor, Tina Rocha, and to proofreaders Merralee Boyce and Colette Weber.

Photo Credits

Brian Holt, underworld, Toledo, Ohio: Cues and cue parts.
Bill Newsted, Bowling Green, Ohio: Buying tests.
Stephen Mayhew: Buying tests.

Preface

This book exists to fill or at least narrow a gap in the pool canon. To my knowledge, there are no books currently available about how to buy a pool cue. Nor are there any books that address in much detail the anatomy of a cue and the different cue construction techniques and materials used by modern cuemakers. There are plenty of books on how to play pool, but these rarely provide much information on cues (Jack Koehler's *The Science of Pocket Billiards* is a notable exception to this rule, offering nearly ten pages of useful information on cues and tips on how to choose one).

The material in *The Pool Cue Book* came primarily from a series of in-depth cuemaker interviews I have been doing for *All About Pool* magazine since 1995 (other research sources are listed in the bibliography). I began interviewing cuemakers because I wanted to learn about cues (and as stated above, no books on cues were yet available). I expected those interviews to resolve all the unanswered questions and conflicting theories on cue design and performance I had encountered in discussions with pool players. In that expectation I was disappointed.

Interviewing cuemakers has not shown me "the truth" about pool cues. Instead, I've learned that there is much diversity of opinion among cuemakers regarding what makes a good-hitting cue and the right or best ways to build cues. This lack of consensus is reflected in the following pages by phrases like "most cuemakers believe that . . ."; "many cuemakers contend that . . ." ; and "some cuemakers hold that . . ." The words most, many and some are used to indicate the degree of consensus among cuemakers as to the validity of the idea or topic under discussion. This is as close to "the truth" as I have been able to get, so far.

While *The Pool Cue Book* is not the definitive book on pool cue performance and construction (that book has yet to be written), it will, I hope, fulfill its objectives. What are those objectives? To provide you, the reader, with: 1) a knowledge of how to go about buying a cue, 2) an understanding of the current, albeit often conflicting, theories on cue performance, and 3) an appreciation of the different construction methods and materials used by modern cuemakers.

Stephen Mayhew
May 12, 1997
Bowling Green, Ohio

Table of Contents

Introduction

There are over 42 million pool players in America, and more and more of them are striding into pool rooms with their own two-piece cues. Priced from $15 to over $100,000, the selection of cues available today is greater than ever. But how do you know which cue is right for you? Here is a cue buying primer designed to give you the knowledge you will need to find that special cue, a cue that will help you run more balls and win more games.

In purchasing a cue, both performance and build quality must be assessed. Performance is a function of the cue's hit and playability. The term *hit* is widely used to describe a cue's performance and feel, i.e., the cue's effect on the cue ball and its feedback to the shooter. For the purposes of this book, hit is defined as a cue's characteristic performance and feedback on medium-speed, center-ball shots. The term *playability* is used to refer to a cue's performance and feedback throughout the range of playing situations, i.e., shots with draw, follow, or English, as well as hard and soft shots. *Build quality* is a function of materials used in the cue and the skill and precision with which those materials are put together. Both performance and build quality will be addressed in detail in the pages that follow.

This book is divided into two parts. *Part I: Why, What, Where, How,* addresses the cue buying basics of why to buy, what to buy, where to buy and how to buy. *Part II: Anatomy of a Two-Piece Cue,* addresses each part of the cue in turn, from the tip to the bumper. Length, weight, and balance are also addressed. Part II is intended to familiarize readers with the different materials and construction techniques used by cuemakers. Throughout the book, informational topics are followed by comments by Mark Kulungian (introduced below) and by tests for assessing performance and build quality as they relate to the particular topic under consideration.

Mark Kulungian is well versed in the principles of pool cue purchasing. He is the owner/operator of Pool Table Magic in Enfield, Connecticut, a 14-table pool room and billiard center offering pool table sales and service and a wide selection of cues, cases, accessories, and instructional materials. He is also a certified BCA instructor and accomplished player. Mark has been buying, selling, and trading cues for over 20 years. His first cue store, which he opened in 1978 to finance his education at West Virginia University, was called George's Billiard Supply, in honor of famed cuemaker George Balabushka. Mark opened Pool Table Magic in 1989.

Mark Kulungian, Cue Aficionado

Mark's area of specialization is vintage and high-end custom cues. He has been a serious collector and dealer of custom cues since 1978, when he bought his first Herman Rambow and Brunswick Hoppe model cues. Mark knows most of the current custom cuemakers and offers for sale one of the widest selections of collectible cues on the east coast, including work by: George Balabushka, Ernie Gutierrez (Ginacue), Paul Mottey, Herman Rambow, Paul Rubino, Bill Schick, Bert Schrager, Tim

Scruggs, Burton Spain, Bill Stroud (Josswest), Gus Szamboti, and Barry Szamboti.

Mark's role in this volume will be to voice, as a knowledgeable and experienced player and buyer and seller of cues, his personal opinions about cue performance and quality. In many respects, Mark's views represent the most commonly accepted version of "the truth" about cues. Commonly accepted, however, does not mean universally accepted. The author will therefore undertake to present all sides of issues where differences of opinion currently exist, without endorsing specific views.

And now, without further ado, let's learn something about pool cues!

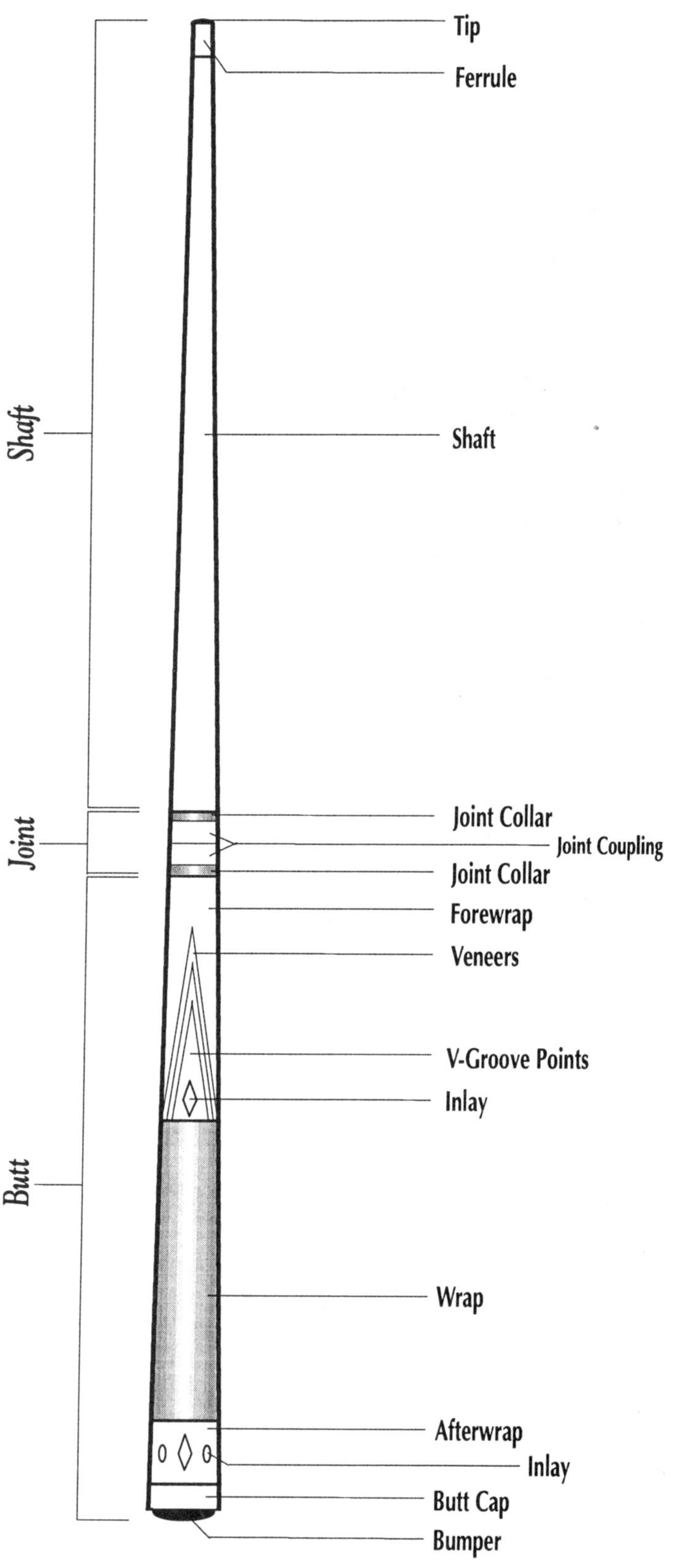
Shaft
Joint
Butt
Tip
Ferrule
Shaft
Joint Collar
Joint Coupling
Joint Collar
Forewrap
Veneers
V-Groove Points
Inlay
Wrap
Afterwrap
Inlay
Butt Cap
Bumper

Part I: Why, What, Where, How

Why to Buy

Predictability

The best reason for a player to own a cue is predictability of performance. Cue performance varies from cue to cue. Pool is a game of variables: speed of shot, speed of cloth, condition of cushions, and so forth. Owning your own cue removes the variable of cue performance from the mix. Once familiar with the performance parameters of your cue, it is easier to predict how hard or soft, or how far off center, you will need to hit the cue ball to achieve the amount of throw, draw, follow or side spin needed for a given shot.

Confidence

Confidence is related to cue predictability. A player's confidence in his or her ability to make a shot is enhanced if the player can predict how the cue will perform in a given situation.

Compatibility

Just as every cue is different, every player is different. Most players learn to adapt their stroking and playing style to the performance characteristics of the cue they are using. It makes more sense, however, to find a cue that fits your style of play. If that cue is not a house cue, or a cue you can rent at the room where you play, then cue ownership is an important step in improving and optimizing your game.

Pride of ownership

It feels good to own a good cue!

What to Buy

Pool cues are available in two basic types: production and custom.

Production Cues

Production cues are made by high-volume manufacturers like Dufferin, McDermott, Viking, and Meucci. These companies make tens of thousands of cues a year. They offer a wide variety of standard models priced from about $75 to $3,000. Production cues are widely available and feature a limited range of options, including tip diameter, weight, wrap material, and a variety of wood stains.

Custom Cues

The term "custom cue" is used rather loosely in the cue industry. All cuemakers and manufacturers call their cues "custom", but there is nothing unique or made-to-order about a cue design that's been repeated thousands of times. While special order cues are available from some manufacturers, truly custom cues are usually the work of smaller companies, one-person shops or small groups of craftspeople turning out from fifty to a few hundred hand-made cues a year. Many custom shops make only one-of-a-kind cues, while others also offer limited production runs of special models. Prices range from about $600 to $5,000, though the sky is the limit in custom cuemaking today, with some cues priced at over $100,000!

The primary advantage of buying a custom cue, aside from originality of aesthetic design, is that your cue can be tailored to your needs. Weight, length, balance point, tip diameter, shaft taper, butt profile, joint design, wrap style – if you know what you want, a custom cuemaker can make it for you, within limits. What are those limits? The cuemaker's personal standards of performance and aesthetics. One should not expect a cuemaker to make a cue that looks or plays like another cuemaker's cues.

Both custom cuemakers and large cue manufacturers aim for consistency in the hit and playability of their cues. A Meucci plays like a Meucci, but differently than a McDermott. A Viking plays like a Viking, but differently than a CueTec, and so forth. Although the differences may be minor, the characteristic hit of each manufacturer's and custom cuemaker's products derives from the different cuemaking philosophies and methods they have adopted.

Kulungian: *To find a good two-piece cue under $50 is nearly impossible. I encourage players to wait to buy their first cue until they have $75 to $150 to spend. For that price, you can buy a good cue made of quality materials that will stay straight and give you good service for many years. You will also be getting something that will hold some of its value if you ever want to sell it to move up to a nicer cue. Dufferin, Mali and others offer good dollar value and quality workmanship under $150.*

From $150 to $700, you've got Meucci, McDermott, Viking, Adams, Falcon and many others. They all make very good cues. In this price range, it's just a question of finding the hit and look that you prefer. At about $600 to $800, you can start considering a custom cue.

Whatever you spend on a cue, what you want to discover is the hit and play characteristics that best suit your game, based on your stance, your stroke, and your style of play. Purchasing a cue is a very personal thing. You want to find a salesperson who's open-minded enough to show you a wide variety of cues and educate you on what you're buying.

Where to Buy

Pool rooms

Many pool rooms offer a limited selection of new and used cues. Some rooms feature pro shops with extensive offerings.

Retailers

Most retailers that sell cues also sell pool tables, cases and accessories. Buyers are likely to find a good selection of cues across a wide price range.

Many pool rooms and retailers do not offer cues priced over $200, as this figure represents the upper price limit of the mass market for cues. Consequently, it can be difficult to find higher-end production cues in stores. Custom cues are even more difficult to locate. Prospective cue buyers should not be surprised if they have to drive to the closest large city to find a good selection of higher-end cues.

Catalogs

The pool specialty catalogs offer wide selection and low prices and are a good alternative, if you already know what you want. The disadvantage of catalog buying is that you cannot try out the cues. This disadvantage also applies to ordering a cue from a manufacturer's or distributor's catalog through a pool room or retailer.

Sporting goods and department stores

Forget 'em. These stores usually offer only low-priced, imported cues of inferior quality. (Note: never buy a cue that breaks down into three or more pieces, unless it's a jump-break cue!)

Trade shows

Trade shows are an excellent place to shop for a cue, particularly custom cues. Trade shows draw some of America's best custom cuemakers and provide buyers with an outstanding selection of cues.

Direct from cuemakers

If you are interested in a particular cuemaker's work, call him up! Many custom shops do a majority of their business by telephone and fax. For cuemaker listings and telephone numbers, consult the *Blue Book of Pool Cues* by Brad Simpson, the *Billiard Encyclopedia* by Victor Stein and Paul Rubino, pool magazines, or contact the American Cuemakers Association (ACA).

From Others

Used cues cost less and are widely available. *Caveat emptor.*

Before you go shopping, ask your pool pals about local places to buy cues. Find out who has the best selection, the most knowledgeable sales people, and the best reputation for honesty and service (remember that the best price is not always the best deal).

How To Buy

Here are some standard procedures to use and ideas to consider when embarking on the purchase of a new cue.

Start with a production cue

Most players' first cue is a production model. Novice players usually have not been playing long enough to really know what kind of hit and playability they want or need in a cue. It takes time and experience to learn to appreciate the differences in the hit of different cues. It's better to spend less money on a production "starter stick" before moving up to a more expensive production or custom cue.

Buy (North) American

One area where the United States still leads the world is in pool cue making, although excellent sticks are also made in Canada. Europe produces many fine cues but these are generally designed for playing billiards or snooker, not pool. Billiard cues are usually shorter and lighter than pool cues. Many of the low-priced cues imported from Asia are of lower quality, some featuring ramin wood shafts instead of the preferred maple and points and inlays that are really only decals. Cues manufactured in Japan by Dick Helmstetter are a notable exception to that rule.

Try a lot of cues

Experience as many cues as you can: house cues, friends' cues, strangers' cues (but always ask first!). Experiment with cues with different tips, different shaft tapers, different joints, different woods. Differences in hit and playability are often subtle. The only way to learn to distinguish them is through experience. One of the best things about buying your own cue is that it will give you a baseline for comparison in assessing the performance of other cues.

Get competent help

It is important for inexperienced cue buyers to find competent help, either from a salesperson or a knowledgeable pool pal. Ask salespeople how long they have been playing pool and selling cues. Test them with the knowledge you glean from this book. Beware of anyone who tries to steer you toward a particular brand of cue before discussing your needs and experience.

Don't zero in on one feature

From a marketing standpoint, it makes sense for cuemakers and manufacturers to tout the superiority of a particular joint design, shaft profile, or construction technique, just as automobile makers tout engines, suspensions, and theft deterrent systems. Remember, however, that a cue is more than a collection of parts. Just as with a car, everything has to work together to get you where you want to go. It is difficult, if not impossible, to attribute the hit of a cue to any single part of it.

Check the warranty

If a problem is going to develop with a cue, it will usually happen within the first few weeks. Most of the major manufacturers warrant their cues against defects in workmanship and materials. Some custom cuemakers guarantee their cues for life. Ask about the warranty before you buy. Also, ask around the pool hall for information on the different manufacturers' reputations for handling warranty claims.

Evaluate performance

To evaluate a cue, you must play with it. To play with a cue – to execute shots with draw, follow, and English – you must chalk the tip. Don't accept a salesperson's "You chalk it, you bought it." If the seller doesn't want you to chalk the tip and doesn't have a chalked demonstrator shaft from the manufacturer that fits the cue, go elsewhere.

More money does not buy more cue

The largest cash prize ever won at a pool tournament – a $1,000,000 bounty for running 10 consecutive racks of 9-ball – was won by Earl Strickland with a $150 cue. More money doesn't buy more cue performance, it generally just buys a prettier cue. High-quality, excellent-hitting cues are widely available for under $200.

Kulungian: *I find that a lot of new buyers overanalyze the process. Remember, pool is a game of feel. You need to buy what feels best to you, not what 'Fast Freddie' down at the pool hall recommended.*

Tests: Take three or four cues that you are interested in and try them out. Set up the same shot and execute it several times with each cue. Start with center ball shots to evaluate the basic hit of the cue before moving on to shots with follow, draw, and English. When you have narrowed your selection to two or three cues, run some balls with each to see which one is the best match for your stroke and style of play.

The Kulungian Blindfold Method

The biggest mistake cue buyers make is to base buying decisions on looks rather than feel and performance. Just because a cue looks great doesn't mean that it hits great or that it's right for you. Here's an easy method to avoid letting the looks of a cue blind you to its potential performance or suitability flaws.

Kulungian: *Go to a cue dealer and select five or six cues in your price range that you like the looks of and that you'd be happy to own. Don't pay any attention to weight or shaft taper or anything else. Just pick the ones that look good to you. Then take the cues to a table and close your eyes. Ask the salesperson to hand you a cue and, with your eyes still closed, get a feel for the weight, the shaft diameter, the grip. Try some practice strokes. How does the cue feel? Then have the salesperson hand you a different cue. Try it out the same way and compare it to the first. Which do you prefer? Go through the same routine with each cue you selected, keeping your eyes closed all the while, and by a process of elimination, you will find the weight, balance, and proportions that are best for you.*

I learned about the closed-eye buying test from the fellow who sold me my first cue over 20 years ago. The cue I use today is within half an ounce of that first one I bought "blindfolded".

A lot of people buy a cue with their eyes, and that's not the way to do it. Pool is a game of feel, so you need to find a cue that feels good to you. After you've found a cue that feels good, you can put it through the tests for hit, straightness, and build quality. The important thing is to find a tool that you're comfortable with.

Checking for Straightness

To play properly, a cue needs to be reasonably straight. Remember that cues are made of wood, an organic material, so don't expect perfect straightness, particularly in the shaft. Also be aware that a shaft or butt may have a compound taper, as opposed to a straight taper. A shaft or butt with a straight taper is shaped like a wedge. It increases in diameter consistently, i.e., in a straight line. A compound taper is, essentially, two or more different straight tapers joined together. A shaft with a compound taper may grow in diameter very slowly through the first several inches and then grow much faster in diameter toward the joint.

Checking for straightness: roll the shaft on the table.

Kulungian: *Now keep in mind, we're talking about something that's about five feet long, less than a half inch in diameter at one end and an inch and a half in diameter at the other, so it's not going to be perfect. It's virtually impossible to make a perfectly jet straight cue over a span of five feet.*

Tests: Roll the shaft on the bed of a slate pool table. Does the shaft roll evenly or does it wobble? Wobbling means a warped shaft. Since most table beds have three pieces of slate, do your test on one end, where you will be rolling the shaft on a single piece of slate. Also, make sure the bed of the table is clean. Bits of chalk, for example, can make a shaft or butt wobble. Get your eyes down at table level and roll the shaft again. Do not expect the shaft to roll flat on the table, unless it has a constant taper. Most pool cue shafts have a "pro" taper, so you will see some light between the tipward area of the shaft and the table. If the light you see is reasonably consistent as you roll the shaft, the shaft is straight. Again, don't expect perfection. A slight inconsistency in the light passing under the shaft is acceptable. (Also, a slight inconsistency might indicate a minor irregularity in concentricity resulting from the shaft being sanded a little too much in one area; such irregularities would have no effect on straightness.)

A constant taper shaft (upper) will roll flat on the table. With a pro taper shaft (lower) some light will be visible between the shaft and the cloth.

Conduct the same tests with the butt. If the butt has a compound taper, you may see some light between the butt and the surface of the table. That's all right, as long as it's consistent. If you see light, dark, light, dark, the butt may be warped. Examine the wrap to see if ridges or bumps are causing the problem.

Checking for straightness: roll the butt on the table.

After you have tested the butt and shaft for straightness, screw the cue together and apply the same tests. (A good place to conduct this test is on a 6'x12' snooker table because the entire cue can be rolled on a single piece of slate.) If the shaft rolls flat and the butt rolls flat, but they do not roll flat together, you have a facing problem at the joint. The other way to test for a facing problem is to unscrew the cue half a turn and then roll it. If it rolls flat that way but wobbles when screwed tightly together, there is a facing problem.

Some cuemakers feel that the best test for straightness is to examine the screwed together cue while slowly rolling it with the

Checking for straightness: roll the cue on the table.

Checking for straightness: roll the cue with the tip on the table and the butt on the rail.

tip on the table and the end of the butt on a rail. If no wobbles are apparent, the cue is reasonably straight. This method eliminates the potential problems of uneven table slates, debris on the table, and wrap imperfections mentioned above.

Part II: Anatomy of a Two-Piece Cue

Although we are talking about two-piece cues, this section will be broken down into three parts: The Shaft, The Joint, and The Butt. Because the joint is part of both the shaft and the butt, it is handy to address it as a separate section of the cue.

The Shaft

The shaft comprises the tip, the ferrule, and the shaft proper. The performance characteristics of a cue are largely determined by its shaft. In light of the importance of the shaft and the number of shaft-related topics that need to be addressed, material relating to the shaft proper will be broken down into three sections: Wood Characteristics and Quality; Construction Considerations; and Performance Considerations. But we begin with a consideration of the tip and ferrule.

The Tip

It's bad news for cue aficionados, but the tip is considered by many to be the most important part of a cue. A $10 house cue with a properly groomed tip will outperform an ivory-inlaid, jewel-encrusted $25,000 custom cue with a poorly maintained tip. A bad tip on a good cue is like bald tires on a race car.

To carry the tire analogy a little further, both tips and tires provide user control through contact patches, with the cue ball and road, respectively. And just as switching from one tire brand or model to another can significantly alter the handling characteristics of a car, switching to a different type of tip can alter the hit and playability of a cue.

Tips are made of leather and range in density from soft to hard. Soft tips tend to mushroom, require more frequent grooming to retain their shape (a tip should have the curvature of a quarter, nickel or a dime), and require more frequent replacement. Some players believe that a softer tip increases the amount of time the tip stays in contact with the cue ball and thus increases cue ball control and action, i.e., effect from hitting the cue ball off center. The sides of a tip that is too soft, however, will tend to collapse when striking a ball with English.

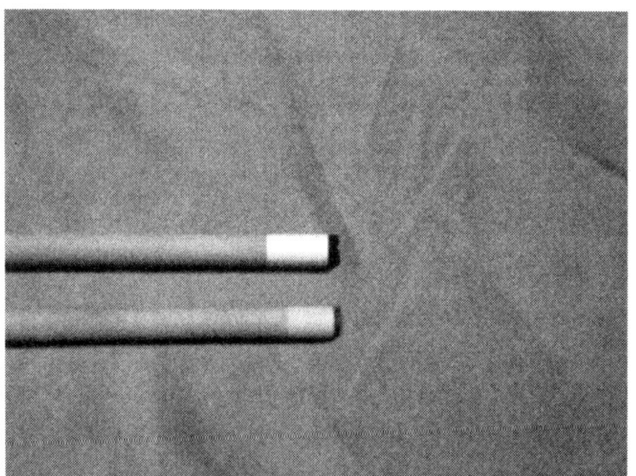

The Tip. A properly groomed tip has straight, burnished sides and the curvature of a quarter, nickel or dime.

Harder tips resist mushrooming, require less grooming to retain their shape, and last longer (often years). Harder tips may need to be scuffed more frequently to get them to hold chalk properly. Many players, including many professionals, prefer medium-hard to hard tips because they hold their shape better than softer tips, thus enhancing shot-to-shot consistency of performance.

Tip diameters range from about 12 to 14 millimeters, with 13 being the most popular. Tip diameter is essentially a question of personal preference. Many accomplished players prefer smaller tips, arguing that they allow a more precise point of aim on the cue ball. A smaller tip is also thought to provide a more precise point of contact on the cue ball, although the curvature of the tip – quarter, nickel, dime – is believed by some to be the determining factor in precision of contact.

Kulungian: *It's a little easier to put action on the cue ball with a smaller tip, even inadvertently! You need to be more accurate in your point of aim on the cue ball with a smaller tip because it will amplify your mistakes. With a larger tip, you need a better stroke to put action on the cue ball, but you have a slightly larger margin of error in your cue ball contact point.*

Tests: Look for straight, well-burnished sides and the curvature of a quarter, nickel, or dime on top. Test hardness by pressing a fingernail into the tip. With a medium-hard to hard tip, your fingernail will make little or no impression.

The Ferrule

The ferrule protects the end of the shaft from splintering. In America they are typically white or cream-colored, while in Canada they tend to be black. In England, snooker cues often feature brass ferrules. Ferrules typically range in length from .5 to 1.25 inches. Billiard cues tend to have shorter ferrules than pool cues.

Ferrule Materials

Ferrule materials include: ivory, buckhorn, bone, and synthetics such as fiber, linen phenolic, melamine, and ABS. Ivory, the traditional ferrule material of choice, has been supplanted by synthetics on most production cues for cost and availability reasons. It is still standard on many custom cues and available as an option from most cuemakers and manufacturers. Ivory is more resistant to chalk staining than most synthetics. Unfortunately, it is also more susceptible to cracking and chipping, due largely to its high water content and its tendency to expand or shrink when the weather changes (the same concerns apply to ivory joint couplings and butt caps). To protect ivory ferrules, many cuemakers use a fiber backing between the tip and the ferrule. Some cuemakers insist that ivory ferrules perform better than synthetics, while others hold that the differences are negligible.

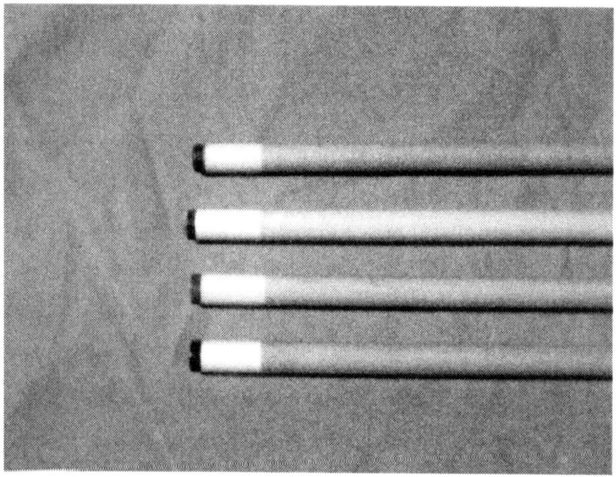

The Ferrule. Different ferrule materials (top to bottom): Fiber, Ivorine III, a linen-based melamine; Linen-based melamine; Ivory.

Types of Ferrules

In terms of design, there are two basic types of ferrules: through and crowned. The standard method of attaching a ferrule to a shaft is with a tenon. The end of the shaft is turned down to create a tenon over which the ferrule is fitted.

With a *through ferrule,* the tenon of the shaft goes all the way through the ferrule, i.e., the ferrule is a hollow tube. With this design, the tip is glued directly to the wood of the shaft, which some cuemakers contend improves the hit and feel of the cue. With a *crowned ferrule,* (also called solid-top, capped or blind ferrule) the tenon of the shaft does not go all the way through the ferrule. Instead, the ferrule has a solid cap or crown to which the tip is glued. Cuemakers using this design argue that it eliminates the possibility of the tenon forcing the tip off the shaft when the wood expands with climate changes. Some cuemakers who use ivory ferrules feel that the crowned design helps prevent chipping and cracking.

The variables of ferrule material, type, length, wall thickness, and attaching method – threaded or non-threaded – allow cuemakers to meet their desired ferrule performance and durability criteria. (Note: ferrules that are threaded on and glued to the shaft tenon should not be confused with "screw-on, screw-off" tips, which are never used on high-quality cues.)

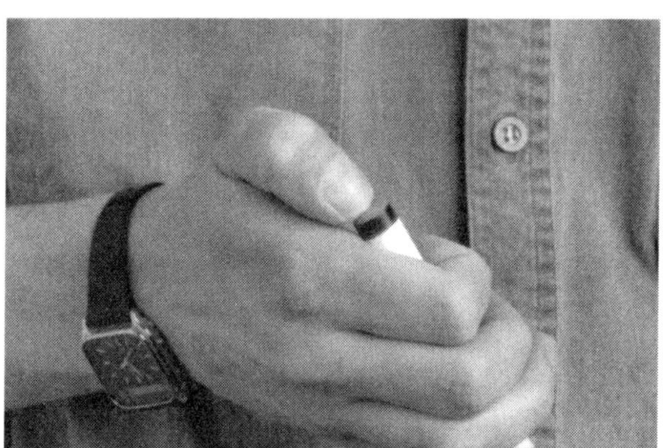

Test tip hardness by pressing a fingernail into the tip.

Kulungian: *Gaps, glue lines and ridges between the ferrule and shaft indicate poor quality construction. These are not simply cosmetic problems. A poorly-fitted ferrule will break down and loosen over time.*

Tests: Check the ferrule for cracks or chipping. Examine the ferrule-shaft joint to make sure there are no gaps or glue lines. Rub your finger over the ferrule-shaft joint to check for ridges; it should be smooth.

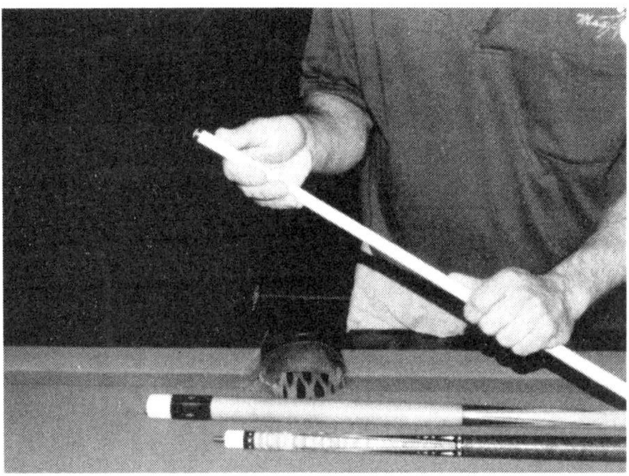

Check the ferrule - shaft joint for smoothness.

The Shaft--
Wood Characteristics & Quality

After the tip, the shaft is considered to be the most important part of a cue in determining its performance characteristics. A variety of factors must be considered in selecting a shaft.

Species of Wood

One area of consensus among pool cue makers and manufacturers is that the wood of choice for pool cue shafts is maple. Shafts have also been made of birch, purpleheart, and other hardwoods, but these are exceptions to the maple rule. Ramin wood is frequently used as a look-alike substitute for maple in very inexpensive cues. English ash is the wood of choice for snooker cue shafts in Europe, but is seldom seen in pool cues.

There are two types of maple: hard and soft. Soft maple is not appropriate for use in shafts. There are two species of hard maple:

sugar maple and black maple. Pool cue shafts are made of sugar maple, also called rock maple, hard rock maple, Canadian rock maple, or Canadian white maple. Sugar maple trees grow throughout much of the eastern United States and Canada. Much of the maple used in shafts comes from Vermont, up-state New York, northern Michigan, and the southern regions of Ontario and Quebec.

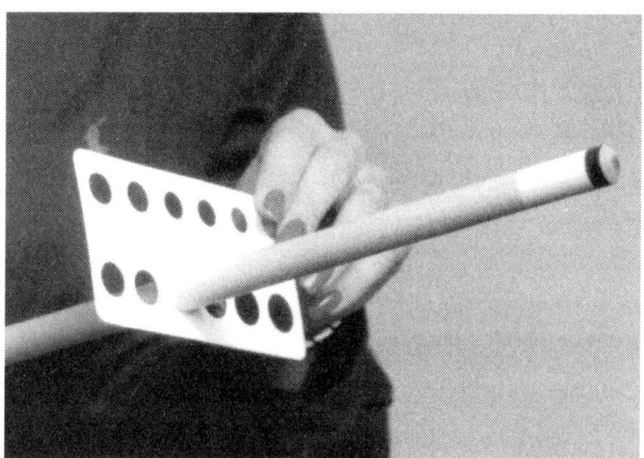

Run a tip gauge up a pro taper shaft to determine the speed of its taper.

Grain

Hard maple can be either straight grained or figured. Figured maple – bird's-eye, curly, fiddleback – is rarely used in shafts because it is usually not as stable as straight-grain maple and tends to warp. (Figured maple is, however, one of the most popular woods used in the forewrap of cues.) There are three factors to consider in the grain of shaft wood: straightness, uniformity, and tightness. All three may affect shaft performance.

Grain is *straight* if the grain lines run straight along the length of the shaft. Grain is *uniform* if the grain lines are evenly spaced across the width of the shaft. Consistency in the straightness and uniformity of grain in a shaft is believed to translate into consistency of performance. Consequently most cuemakers agree that straightness and uniformity of grain, especially through the first 6 to 18 inches back from the tip, are the most important criteria in shaft wood selection. These factors may also contribute to a shaft's ability to resist warping and remain straight over a period of many years.

Tightness of grain refers to how close together the grain lines are across the width of the shaft. Grain lines are actually the growth rings of the tree from which the shaft was made. In maple, the number of growth rings can range anywhere from 4 to 32 per inch, with more rings indicating the slower growth of northern climates. Shaft wood should usually have at least eight growth rings per inch.

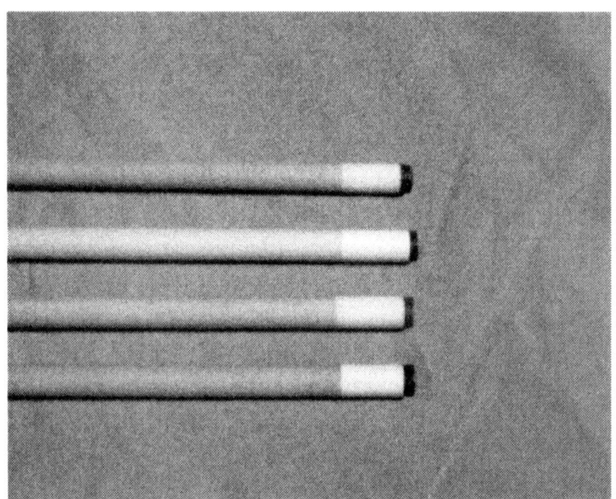

The Shaft. Different tightnesses of grain.

Many cuemakers believe there is a relationship between tightness of grain and shaft weight and density. Generally, tighter grain produces heavier, denser shafts, although the relationship is by no means direct, i.e., exceptions to the rule are common. A similar relationship is believed to exist between shaft density and stiffness. Generally, a heavier, denser shaft will be stiffer than a lighter shaft of the same dimensions, though again, the relationship is not direct. Some cuemakers feel a shaft should weigh at least four ounces, while others offer lighter shafts, sometimes to meet player preferences in shaft performance.

Many cuemakers prize tightly-grained shaft wood, and the tighter the better. Others use varying degrees of tightness of grain to help achieve varying degrees of stiffness or flexibility in their shafts. Still others hold that tightness of grain has little to do with shaft performance and that the real issue is the cell structure of the wood, of which there are no reliable visual indicators. Overall, straightness and uniformity of grain are considered by most cuemakers to be more important than tightness of grain in producing high-quality shafts.

Color

Shaft color ranges from nearly white to light brown. Most shafts are made from sap wood, as opposed to the darker heartwood of the tree. The color of the wood is determined by several factors, including growing locale, harvesting season, and drying methods. Wood harvested in summer is more likely to have dark sugar lines (crystallized sap), especially if it is subjected to heat after cutting. Harvested maple will also darken if left out in the rain. Winter harvesting helps avoid these problems. The low-temperature dehumidifier and vacuum kiln methods of drying usually produce the best results. Faster, high temperature drying methods tend to darken the wood and can damage its cell structure, resulting in inferior shaft quality and performance.

Some cuemakers hold that whiteness is an important indicator of maple that has been properly harvested and processed for use in shafts. Others do not feel that color is a significant factor in shaft selection. Color does seem to be an important factor in the cue market, where very white shafts are often prized.

Clarity

The clarity or cleanliness of shaft wood is primarily a cosmetic consideration. Mineral streaks, dark sugar lines, and other blemishes are common in maple. In terms of performance, these imperfections are of little consequence, although if found toward the tip of the cue, they may be a distraction in aiming. At any rate, most minor blemishes are quickly masked as a shaft is used and a smooth patina of chalk dust and oil from the player's hand builds up.

Several factors are affecting the availability and price of top-grade shaft wood. Demand for maple shaft wood has increased dramatically in Europe and Asia, and domestically as well. Only a small amount of maple that is harvested is appropriate for cue shafts. Maple is a slow-growing wood, and the best maple for shaft wood grows in northern climates where the growing season is short. This all leads to two conclusions: 1) players may soon have to start paying a premium for top-grade shafts (some custom cue-makers now charge $300 for a shaft); and 2) players may have to overlook minor cosmetic blemishes in shafts.

The Shaft -- Construction Considerations

Seasoning

All woods used in cues need to be seasoned before they are used. Seasoning or aging is necessary to make sure that the wood is adequately and uniformly dry. Improperly seasoned wood in a cue will tend to shrink, check, or warp as the drying process is completed after the cue is finished. Ebony, for example, a heavy, dense wood, is notorious for checking and shrinking if not properly seasoned before use. With the maple used for shafts, warping is the main problem. If the maple is not uniformly dry, some areas of the shaft will be more dense than others, resulting in inconsistent performance.

How long maple shaft wood should be aged is a question of opinion. Legendary cuemakers George Balabushka and Gus Szamboti aged their shaft wood for years, taking up to five years to finish a shaft. Hall of Fame cuemaker Burton Spain, on the other hand, felt that a year's aging was plenty long enough.

Another reason cuemakers season shaft wood is to allow the wood to reach a settled equilibrium with the relative humidity of the shop, which may or may not be climate controlled. Wood takes on or gives off moisture until it reaches an equilibrium with the relative humidity of its surroundings. It is important that shaft wood be in this state of equilibrium before it is turned.

Turning

Turning is the process of cutting a shaft on a lathe. Most cuemakers agree that a shaft should be turned down to finished size gradually through a series of small cuts over a period of months or years. Even properly-seasoned wood has *internal tension*, which we can define as a tendency to orient itself in a particular direction. Wood from a tree that grew on the side of a hill and had to bend toward the sunlight will have more internal tension than wood from a tree that grew straight on level ground.

Incremental turning allows for the gradual stress relief of the internal tension in the shaft wood. After each cut the wood moves or settles into its natural orientation which may or may not be straight along the length of the shaft. With each turning, any slight warping resulting from the settling of the wood after the previous cut is removed. Each cut should yield a smaller and smaller amount of movement in the wood so that by the final cut the shaft's natural orientation is straight.

Some cuemakers use a chemical stabilizing agent on shaft wood during the construction process. The stabilizing agent impregnates the wood fibers and is intended to reduce the chances of warpage by reducing the finished shaft's susceptibility to changes of temperature and humidity. Other cuemakers contend that chemical stabilizing agents are unnecessary and may even detract from a shaft's natural hit and playability.

Taper

The taper of a shaft is its shape or profile. Most tapers fall into two general categories: European or pro. The *European taper*, also called a constant or straight taper, is cone shaped. It grows in diameter continuously from the tip to the joint. European taper shafts are most commonly found on billiard cues. The extra strength and stiffness of the European taper, which derives from its cone shape, helps three cushion billiards players propel larger, heavier balls greater distances, as compared to pool.

The *pro taper* features several inches of cylindricalness before the shaft starts to increase in diameter and take on a wedge or cone shape as it moves toward the joint. Within the pro taper category, there are long pro tapers and short pro tapers. A long pro taper, also called a slow pro taper, features 10 to 14 inches of cylindricalness before the shaft begins to grow in diameter. A short pro taper, also called a fast pro or modified European taper, has six to eight inches of cylindricalness. Pro taper shafts currently dominate the pool cue industry, but many custom cuemakers will accommodate requests for custom tapers.

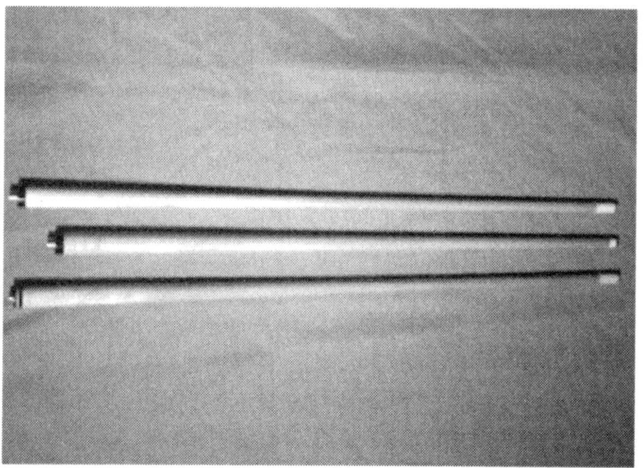

The Shaft. Different tapers, top to bottom: Pro; Constant; Modified European.

Some cuemakers believe that, for strength and consistency of play, a shaft should have at least minimal growth along its entire length. These cuemakers offer "pro" tapers that feel cylindrical, but which actually feature very gradual growth from the ferrule back.

Comfort and ease of follow through are touted as advantages of the cylindricalness of the slow pro taper. With no growth in shaft diameter, the player's bridge does not need to be loosened to allow for follow through. Many billiard players, however, feel that the growth in shaft diameter of a European taper is advantageous for gauging follow through.

The Shaft -- Performance Considerations

Two terms – deflection and squirt – are at the root of any consideration of shaft performance. Unfortunately, a good deal of disagreement surrounds these terms and numerous theories have been proposed to explain their effects on cue performance.

Deflection

When the cue hits the cue ball, the shaft bends. This is called *deflection.* The term deflection is also commonly used to refer to changes in cue ball trajectory when using English (see squirt below); in this book, however, deflection is used only in relation to the shaft. Although the butt of the cue also plays a role, the amount of deflection a cue will have is considered to be primarily a function of how much spine the shaft has.

Spine

Spine is a term used to describe shaft rigidity. How much spine the shaft has determines where it bends when it contacts the cue ball. More spine pushes the center of the bend forward, toward the tip. Because a shorter section of the shaft is bending, the shaft deflects less.

The taper of the shaft is important in determining how much spine it will have. Generally, the longer the taper, the less spine the shaft will have and the more it will deflect. Consequently, a European taper shaft will usually deflect less than a fast pro taper shaft, which will usually deflect less than a slow pro taper shaft.

Many cuemakers feel that the weight and density of the wood in the shaft also play a role in deflection and spine. In this view, a heavier, denser shaft will usually have more spine and deflect less than a lighter shaft. Thus, cuemakers have two tools – wood selection and shaft taper – to determine the performance characteristics of their shafts.

Squirt

With side English, squirt comes into play. Robert Byrne, the author of two of the best-selling instructional books on pool: *Byrne's Standard Book of Pool and Billiards* and *Byrne's Advanced Technique in Pool and Billiards*, defines squirt as the movement off the line of aim of a cue ball struck with English. Left English makes the cue ball squirt to the right, while right English produces squirt to the left. Squirt must be compensated for in aiming.

There are several schools of thought on what kind of shaft produces less squirt. Byrne holds that a stiffer shaft produces less squirt and therefore requires less compensation in aiming. As proof of his theory, he offers *The "Impossible" Cut Shot* on page 120 of *Byrne's Standard Book of Pool and Billiards.* This is a rail-first cut shot in which the cue ball must be struck with extreme English. According to Byrne, with a stiff shaft, i.e., low deflection, the shot can be accomplished with almost no aiming compensation for squirt, while a whippy, i.e., high deflection, shaft requires nearly a ball's width of compensation. Byrne's conclusion: stiff shafts deflect less and produce less squirt than whippy shafts.

Another school of thought, exemplified by Jack H. Koehler in his *The Science of Pocket Billiards*, asserts that high deflection translates into low squirt. Koehler holds that when a cue stick hits a cue ball with English, either the shaft must bend, i.e., deflect, or the cue ball must move, i.e., squirt. According to this theory, because a whippy, high-deflection shaft bends more easily, it will produce less squirt than a stiff shaft and thus require smaller adjustments for squirt in aiming.

As for the direction that the shaft bends when contacting the cue ball, there are two theories. Consider a shot with left English. Some observers hold that the shaft bends to the right, allowing the tip to move off the cue ball to the left. Other observers hold that the shaft bends to the left, creating and arc that keeps the tip in contact with the cue ball. Factors other than shaft rigidity, such as how tightly or loosely the cue is gripped, may be involved in the cue dynamics of shots with English. High-speed photographic studies may be necessary to resolve this debate.

In the August, 1994 issue of *Billiards Digest*, columnist Bob Jewett reported the results of tests to assess squirt. Gluing a tip to a solid aluminum rod about 5/8-inch in diameter, Jewett found that the rod produced about three times more squirt than a normal cue. Shafts with four-inch brass inserts in the tip, provided by Houston cuemaker Jim Buss, produced almost as much squirt as the aluminum rod. To the reader, it would seem logical to conclude that if a zero-deflection, super-stiff rod produces uncontrollable amounts of squirt, then a stiff shaft will produce more squirt than a whippy shaft. However, large amounts of squirt were also produced by an extra long cue with a fairly flexible shaft that Jewett tested.

Jewett concluded that European taper shafts produce about half as much squirt as long pro taper shafts. He added that short pro taper shafts offer much of the ease of stroke of the long pro taper, while still maintaining an acceptable degree of accuracy with side spin. In his column, Jewett recommended the aim and pivot technique to compensate for squirt when using side spin. This technique can also be used to assess the amount of squirt produced by different shaft tapers.

The amount of weight at the tip of the cue may be another piece of the deflection/squirt puzzle. In reference to the Jewett metal rod test, Robert Byrne suggests that extra weight at the tip of the shaft – rather than lack of shaft deflection – was primarily responsible for the large amounts of squirt that Jewett encountered. At least one well-known cuemaker uses a special light-weight tenon and ferrule assembly to minimize weight at the tip of his cues.

Controversy rages over the merits of low-deflection, stiff-hitting shafts versus high-deflection, whippy shafts. With center ball hits, there is probably little difference between a whippy shaft and a stiff one. With draw, follow, and English, many people feel that a whippy shaft will help the player put action on the cue ball. Bob Jewett, on the other hand, contends that from a physics standpoint, the amount of spin put on the cue ball is primarily a function of how far off center it is struck and that the whippiness or stiffness of the shaft makes very little difference in how much action is imparted to the cue ball. No matter what type of shaft a player is using, a smooth, accelerating stroke is considered by many to be the key to putting action on the cue ball.

Consistency

Consistency and predictability are important performance features to consider in a shaft. *Consistency* relates to how a shaft performs on different types of shots, such as hard versus soft. The more consistently a shaft performs throughout the range of shots, the more predictable it is.

A linear relationship between speed of shot and shaft performance would be: a 10 percent harder draw shot produces 10 percent more draw and a 25 percent harder draw shot produces 25 percent more draw. An exponential relationship between speed and performance would be: a 10 percent harder draw shot produces 10 percent more draw, but a 25 percent harder draw shot produces 50 percent more draw. The more linear the relationship between speed of shot and shaft performance, the more consistent and predictable the shaft will be.

Many believe that a stiff, low-deflection shaft will be more consistent and predictable than a whippy, high-deflection shaft. As mentioned in *The Shaft -- Wood Characteristics and Quality*, straightness and uniformity of grain may also affect shaft consistency.

With all the variables to consider in pool – the speed of the cloth, the speed of the bumpers, the tightness of the pockets, the cleanliness of the balls – players, especially novices, might be well-advised to opt for a stiffer, more predictable shaft rather than a whippier, less predictable one. That said, there remains a high degree of disagreement on the performance aspects of both whippy and stiff shafts. There are a host of conflicting theories, other than those presented above, so it behooves players to try as many different shaft designs as possible to find what works best for them.

Kulungian: *Shaft wood is critical. If the shaft has a lot of flex, you're going to get a lot of whippiness when the cue tip contacts the cue ball. A European taper is going to give you a stiffer hit because you've got more wood in the shaft. A stiffer-hitting cue will give you less deflection, and less deflection means more accuracy.*

With a whippy shaft, it's easier to put action -- follow, draw, and English -- on the cue ball, but it's harder to gauge and control the action, that is, to get exactly the amount you want. You need a better stroke to put action on the cue ball with a stiffer shaft, but it's more predictable, and thus more controllable.

Tightness of grain also affects stiffness, so there are ranges of stiffness and flexibility within the different taper categories. Usually, the tighter the grain, the heavier the shaft and the stiffer the hit.

As for the quality of the wood, consistency of grain is the most important consideration. Blemishes in the wood are primarily a cosmetic consideration, unless they are found in the first few inches of the shaft, where they can be distracting to the player in aiming and can affect consistency of shaft performance.

Tests: Examine the shaft for straightness and uniformity of grain. Do the grain lines run reasonably straight along the length of the shaft? Are they spaced evenly across the width of the shaft? Remember that many cuemakers feel that straightness and uniformity of grain are more important in the first six to 18 inches of the shaft than farther back toward the joint.

Check for sugar lines, mineral spots and other blemishes, especially toward the tip. Don't expect perfection.

Look at the taper. Most modern pool cue shafts have a pro taper, but you want to know whether you're buying a long or a short pro taper. Run a tip gauge up the shaft to determine the length of the taper. The farther up the shaft the gauge goes before encountering shaft growth, the longer the pro taper. Compare the shaft to other shafts to get an idea of the different tapers available.

If you're buying a cue with two shafts, you want the weight and grain of the shafts to be as close to each other as possible. Hit with both of them. Be aware, however, that even shafts of identical weight and taper, made from the same piece of wood, will hit slightly differently.

The Joint

The joint comprises the joint collars, the joint coupling, the joint pin, and depending on the design, the shaft insert. The screw in the joint is usually referred to as the *joint pin.* The part of the joint that houses the pin and that fits against the shaft side of the joint is the *joint coupling.* A *shaft insert* is a hollow, threaded piece of metal or plastic that is fitted into the shaft to accept the joint pin.

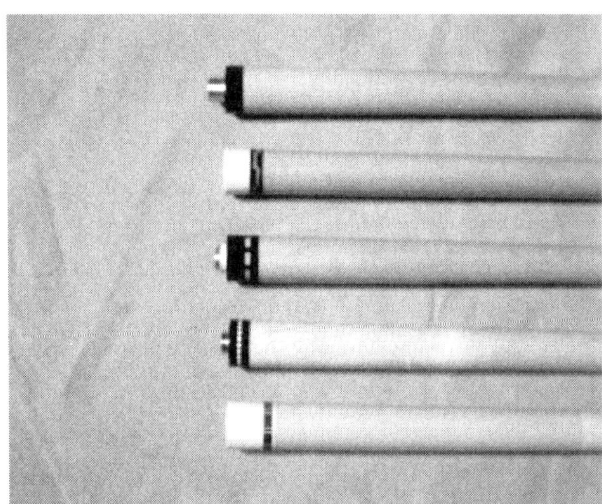

The Joint. Different joint collar treatments.

Many cues feature *joint collars* on either side of the joint coupling, one on the shaft and one on the butt. The joint collar on the shaft acts as a ferrule to protect the edges of the wood from splintering and chipping. The joint collar on the butt side of the joint is primarily decorative. Joint collar materials include ivory, exotic wood, stainless steel, brass, and phenolic and other synthetics. Many cues feature decorative rings in the joint collars.

Types of Joints

A wide variety of joint designs and materials is available on modern cues. Most joint designs, however, fall into two categories: piloted or flat-faced.

Piloted Joints

With a *piloted joint*, a stainless steel, aluminum, or brass insert in the shaft ends with a nipple that fits into a corresponding cavity in the butt. The most common type of piloted joint features a 5/16-14 or 5/16-18 (5/16 inch in diameter; 14 or 18 threads per inch) stainless steel screw and a stainless steel or nickel silver joint coupling. Piloted, all-metal joints are reputed to offer a "harder" hit than other joints, but not all cuemakers endorse that notion. The "hardness" of the all-metal joint hit is said to be "softened" if a phenolic or ivory joint coupling is used.

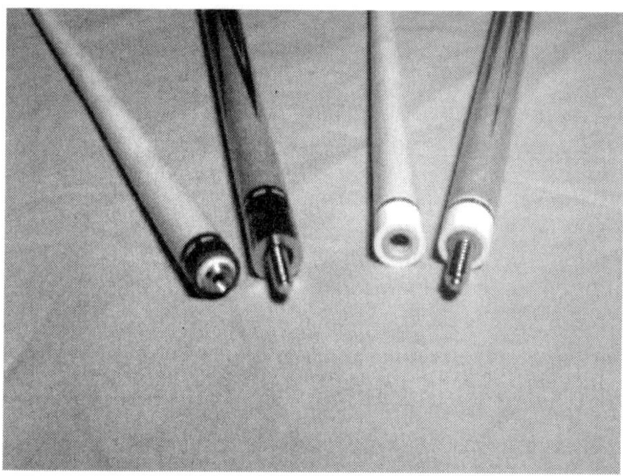

The Joint. Standard designs: Piloted, flat-faced.

Flat-faced Joints

With *flat-faced joints,* there is no nippled insert on the shaft. The joint faces of the butt and shaft fit flat against each other. The most common type of flat-faced joint features a 3/8-10 stainless steel joint pin and corresponding threads cut directly into the wood of the shaft. Another type of flat-faced joint uses a flat-faced shaft insert, usually of plastic or brass, with a 5/16-14 or 5/16-18 stainless steel or brass joint pin. Flat-faced joint coupling options include ivory, brass, stainless steel, wood, and phenolic and other synthetics.

Unlike most piloted joints, the flat-faced design offers wood-to-wood contact at the joint, something which many players prize for its reputedly superior feel and feedback. Flat-faced joints are said to offer a "softer" hit than piloted, metal joints, but again, not all cuemakers agree with that assessment. Cross threading or a burr on the metal screw can damage the wooden threads in the shaft, but with proper care, a 3/8-10 joint will provide many years of service.

Flat-faced joints usually weigh about one to one-and-a-half ounces less than their piloted stainless steel counterparts. This can be a consideration in the weighting and balancing of the cue. Some cuemakers use the weight of an all-metal, piloted joint to move the balance point of their cues forward. Other cuemakers feel that extra weight at the joint detracts from a cue's performance and "natural" balance. Lighter joint coupling options with the piloted design include titanium, ivory, buckhorn, and phenolic and other synthetics.

Other joint designs include the *reverse joint,* where the shaft screws into the butt; the *all-wood joint,* a variety of reverse joint featuring a large-diameter wooden screw that is popular in Europe; the *double-screw joint,* where the shaft and butt screw into each other; and the *Uni-Loc* quick-release joint.

Many cuemakers offer their own joint designs or modified versions of the standard piloted and flat-faced joints. Joe Gold (Cognoscenti) uses a 3/8-10 glass epoxy joint pin. South West cues feature a 3/8-11 brass pin. Mike Lambros uses a standard 3/8-10 pin, but has convex and concave faces on the shaft and butt respectively. Ray Schuler's *interference fit joint* is a piloted design that also features the wood-to-wood contact of a flat-faced joint. Joe Porper, Samsara, Richard Chudy . . . the list of cuemaker-specific joint designs and modified standard joints goes on and on.

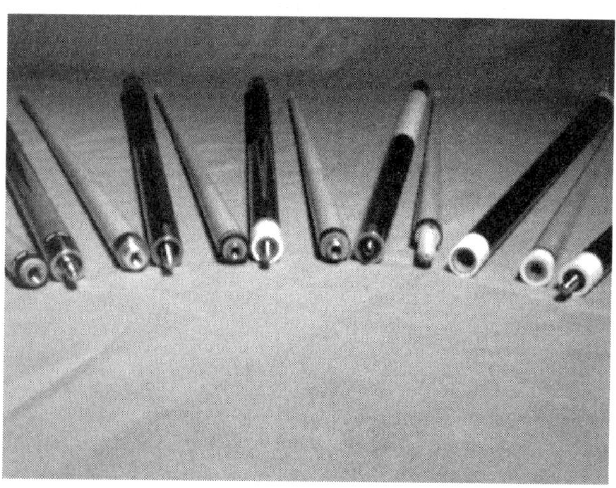

The Joint. Other designs, left to right: Helmstetter "Twin"; Viking double screw; Huebler flat faced with plastic shaft insert; Schuler interference fit; Helmstetter all-wood reverse; Meucci flat-faced with metal insert.

Kulungian: *Each type of joint has its proponents. George Balabushka and Gus Szamboti preferred the stainless steel, piloted joint. Modern master Jerry Franklin of South West Cues preferred the flat-faced, wood-to-wood joint. Some cuemakers don't think the joint design is very important at all, as long as the cue screws tightly together. As a general guideline, I would say that a stainless steel joint produces a harder-hitting cue. Ivory, brass, and the plastics at the joint produce softer-hitting cues. What's important is what the player prefers.*

Check the joint coupling - joint collar for smoothness.

Tests: Run your finger over the joint coupling and joint collars to check for smoothness.

As with the ferrule, check for the absence of gaps, glue lines, and ridges.

Screw the cue together and run your finger over the joint to check for smoothness. You want it to be as smooth as possible.

To check the closeness of the tolerances in the joint, screw the cue almost together and then wiggle the shaft a little. Excessive play indicates that the shaft insert or wooden threads are too big. Inexpensive cues are often built to less exacting tolerances.

The Butt

The butt comprises the forewrap, the wrap area, the afterwrap, the butt cap, and the bumper. The *forewrap,* also called the forearm, front, or nose, is the section of the cue between the joint and the top of the wrap. The *wrap area,* also called the grip or handle, is where the cue is gripped; the *afterwrap,* also called the butt sleeve, is the section of the cue between the end of the wrap and the butt cap. The *butt cap,* also called the butt plate, is the section of the cue at the end of the butt. The *bumper* is the rubber fitting that protrudes from the butt cap to protect the cue when it is stood on the floor.

The butt of the cue is what garners most of the attention, even though the tip and shaft are much more important in determining how the cue will play. The traditional four-prongs-with-veneers design, while still popular, is only one of a huge variety of designs available on modern cues. Six, eight, and twelve-point cues with and without veneers, no-point cues, cues with geometric designs, cues with pictures . . . the possibilities are endless. More important than how a butt looks, however, is how it is built.

Construction Techniques

The butt of a cue can be constructed from one, two or three sections. A *one-piece butt*, also called a merry widow, features one solid piece of wood from the joint to the butt cap. One-piece butts are the simplest to build, but are not appropriate with certain types of wood. Bird's-eye maple, burls, and other randomly-grained woods are inherently unstable and tend to warp when used in 29-inch lengths. (Some cuemakers core out less stable woods and sleeve them onto straight-grain maple, even on shorter lengths, such as a cue forewrap. The same coring technique can be used with heavier woods like ebony to produce lighter cues.)

Two-piece and three-piece butts are the industry standard. *Two-piece butts* feature an internal, permanently sealed joint between the forewrap and the handle or wrap section of the cue. With two-piece butts, the handle section extends to the butt cap. The area below the wrap is often turned down so that other woods and decorative rings can be sleeved onto it (hence the term *butt sleeve*). Most cuemakers use straight-grain maple for the handle section of cues with wraps.

Three-piece butts feature a second internal, sealed joint between the bottom of the wrap and the afterwrap. Two-piece and three-piece construction allows cuemakers and manufacturers to work with a wider variety of woods and designs. In terms of playability, even skilled players would be hard-pressed to notice any difference between two-piece and three-piece butts.

Most cuemakers agree that the joint between the forewrap and the handle is the most important structural factor in producing a good-playing, structurally-sound cue. Several different joining techniques are used: tenons, dowels, wood screws, metal screws, phenolic couplings, and combinations of these. Because of the importance of this joint, some cuemakers are rather secretive about the joining techniques they have developed. On some cues, the decorative phenolic, wood, or metal rings at the top of the wrap also serve a structural purpose: reinforcing the forewrap-handle joint.

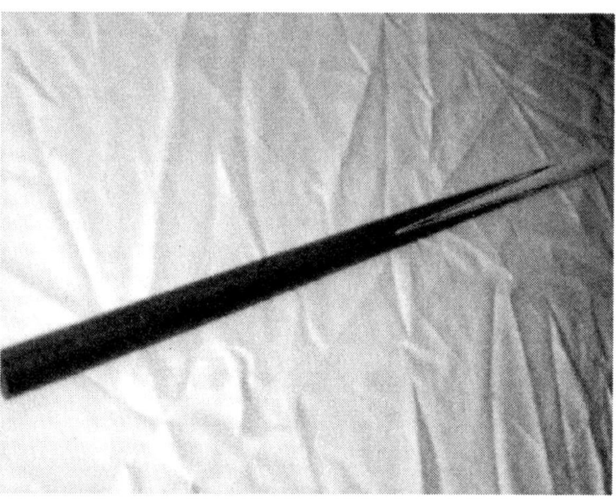

The Butt. Full-splice construction (Hercek).

The integrity of the forewrap-handle joint is also important in avoiding buzzes in the cue. Wood tends to absorb glue and epoxy through the end grain. If the adhesive bond where end grain joins end grain in a cue is broken, the pieces of wood can rub against each other, creating a buzzing sound. All internal, wood-to-wood joints in a cue are subject to buzzing, but the problem occurs most commonly at the forewrap-handle joint. Buzzing in cues, especially high-quality cues, is more often attributable to mistreatment and abuse than to faulty construction.

Points

Points are the triangular design elements commonly found in the forewraps of cues. They are also called prongs or the crown of the cue. There are two basic types of points: spliced and inlaid.

Spliced points serve the structural purpose of joining the forewrap to the handle of the cue. Splicing techniques predate the screw and tenon joining techniques outlined above. Most spliced cues feature two-piece butts, with the wood of the points running through to the butt cap, although other woods and decorative rings can be sleeved on at the afterwrap. The two most common splicing techniques are the four-prong splice and the butterfly splice.

The *four-prong splice* is also called the full splice or finger splice. With this technique, four prongs cut into the handle fit into V-shaped recesses cut into the forewrap of the cue. The V-shaped cuts in the handle extend to the center of the cue at their widest point and become more shallow as the points narrow. Decorative veneers, usually two to five, are often used. The points and veneers of this splice are straight-sided and come to sharp points. The Brunswick *Titlist* and the common house cue are examples of the four-prong splice.

The less frequently seen *butterfly splice* uses a V-splice to join the forewrap to the handle of the cue. A two-point cue has one V-splice; a four-point cue has two V-splices. Another method of obtaining butterfly points, which is not actually a splice, involves building up the butt of the cue from full-length pieces of wood sandwiched together before they are turned down to reveal the "butterflies." The sides of butterfly points are curved and the veneers show more than full-splice veneers and blend into each other. Four-prong and butterfly splices have been used together in cues, as in the famed Brunswick *Model 360.*

While most cuemakers are familiar with traditional splicing techniques, spliced points are rarely used in modern cues (aside from house cues) because they are costly in terms of time and materials. Instead, inlaid points are used. *Inlaid points,* as the name suggests, are inlaid into the forewrap of the cue. They do not serve the structural purpose of joining the forewrap to the handle, as is the case with spliced points. Instead, the forewrap is joined to the handle using the construction techniques outlined above.

Inlaid points are usually easier and less time consuming to execute than spliced points. They can also be executed with much smaller pieces of wood than are required for spliced points (and the exotic hardwoods used in points can be expensive). For example, four inlaid points of Brazilian rosewood might require four .5" x .5" x 9" pieces of wood, i.e., nine cubic inches of exotic wood, while spliced points would require one 1.5" x 1.5" x 23" piece of rosewood, i.e., 51.75 cubic inches of exotic wood, most of which may be covered by a wrap.

In addition to saving time and materials, the screw or screw-and-tenon technique of joining the forewrap to the handle offers cuemakers greater control of weight and balance, and the option of inserting decorative rings between the fore-wrap and the handle. Both the V-groove and butterfly inlaid points discussed below are indistinguishable from spliced points in a wrapped cue.

Inlaid points come in three basic styles: V-groove, flat-bottomed, and butterfly. *V-groove* points, also called mitered, milled, or short-splice points, fit into V-shaped cuts in the fore-wrap of the cue. Where the points join the wrap, the V-shaped cuts extend nearly to the center of the cue. The cuts become more shallow as the points narrow, as with four-prong spliced points. V-groove points usually come to a sharp point at the tip and often feature decorative veneers that also come to sharp points. V-groove points with

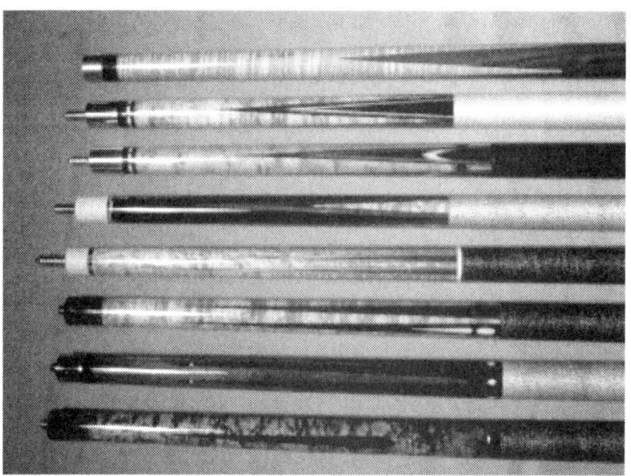

The Butt. Types of points, left to right: Fullsplice (Helmstetter); Full-splice with veneers and wrap (Hercek); V-grove with veneers and inlaid butterflies (Helmstetter); V-grove with veneers (Huebler); V-groove with veneers and decorative ring at top of wrap as structural element (Cousins); Flat-bottomed with inlays (Schuler); Flat-bottomed, capped with inlays (Schuler); Flat-bottomed floating, compound (Schuler).

veneers have been popular for decades and represent a traditional approach to cuemaking, though not quite as traditional as spliced points.

Flat-bottomed points fit into flat-bottomed pockets cut into the forewrap of the cue with a manual pantograph or a computer numeric controlled (CNC) milling machine. This explains why they are also called pantographed or CNC points. These points are slightly rounded at the tips, unless additional hand work is done to "sharpen" them. Flat-bottomed points were introduced in the early 1980's and have gained wide acceptance. They offer design flexibility that is unavailable with traditional V-groove or spliced points.

Two common types of flat-bottomed points are compound points and floating points. *Compound points* are points within points. They are often used to simulate the veneers of V-groove points. *Floating points* are points that do not extend to the wrap. They seem to "float" in the forewrap of the cue. Floating points can be simple or compound. Floating points are a good example of the design flexibility made possible by the introduction of flat-

The Butt. Internal view of V-groove (L) and flat-bottomed (R) points. (Forewraps courtesy of The Schuler Cue.)

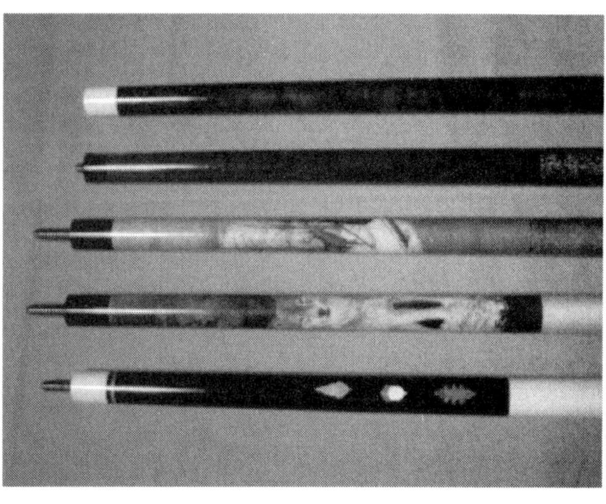

The Butt. Forewrap treatments in non-pointed cues, top to bottom: Stained bird's-eye maple (Helmstetter); Purpleheart (Schuler); Painted scene (McDermott); Painted scene (McDermott); Inlays (Meucci).

bottomed points.

Proponents of V-groove points assert that they are an important structural component that improve the strength and hit of a cue. Proponents of flat bottomed points, on the other hand, contend that the increased gluing surfaces required with V-groove points increase the risk of air pockets and rattles in the forewrap and that points on non-spliced cues are purely a matter of aesthetics. The controversy has raged for years and is not likely to subside any time soon. What is undeniable is that excellent-playing cues are available in either configuration. Many cuemakers offer both V-groove and flat-bottomed points, letting the aesthetic design of the cue dictate the type of points used.

Lightly tap the cue and listen for buzzes, rattles, and hollows.

Like their spliced cousins, butterfly inlaid points are uncommon. *Butterfly inlaid points* use the same techniques as spliced butterfly points, but with a shorter section of wood. The butterfly points are inlaid in the forewrap of the cue, which is then joined to the handle with a tenon or screw-and-tenon technique. As with spliced cues, butterfly inlaid points can be used in conjunction with V-groove points, either between or inside them.

Tests: With a cue with points, hold the butt by the wrap in one hand and lightly tap the prong against your other hand as you rotate the cue, and listen. You should hear the same soft ring as you go around the cue. If you hear a rattle or hollow sound, it means there is an air pocket in the cue where the adhesive bond between materials has broken down. Also, hit with the cue and listen for buzzes.

Check the points. Do they line up evenly? Are the spaces between the points even where they meet the wrap? With V-groove

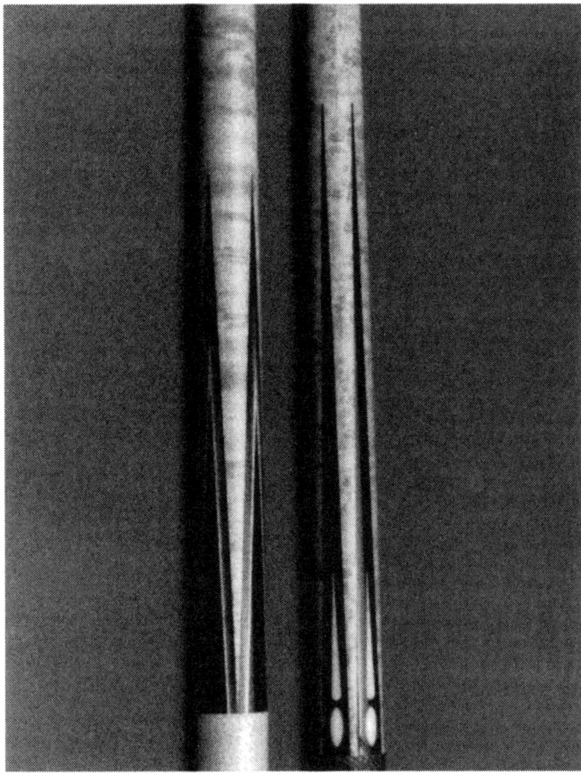

Check the alignment of the points. The tips of flat-bottomed-points (right) should line up close to perfectly. With V-groove points and veneers (left) expect slight imperfections; notice in the photo that the tops of the points line up, but that the inner points are slightly off; this degree of imperfection is well within acceptable tolerances for full-spliced or V-groove points.

points, do the veneers match up with each other and come to sharp points? (Keep in mind that custom cues are hand built, so the points will probably not line up perfectly).

Note: Some cuemakers decry the procedure of whacking an assembled cue against the palm of the hand at the joint or shaft to see how much it vibrates. They hold that this is not a reliable indicator of how the cue will play because resistance to lateral forces is a meaningless criterion when applied to a tool that is designed to work under compression, like a poker. Other cuemakers contend that resistance to lateral forces is of value in assessing a cue's stiffness, structural integrity, and weight distribution.

Note: Hand-made cues are imperfect. A few minor flaws are to be expected, even on cues costing thousands of dollars.

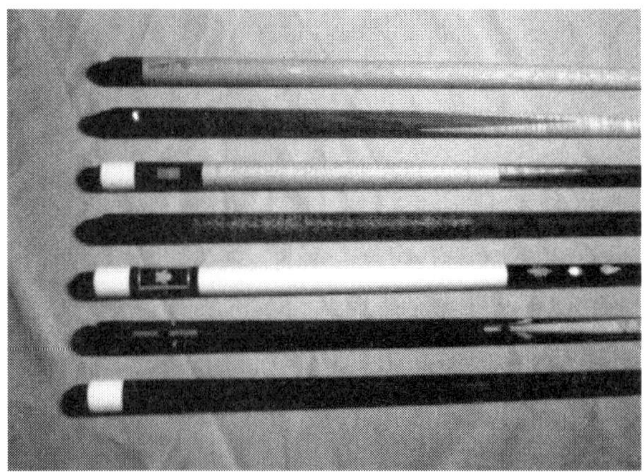

The Butt. Different wraps, top to bottom: No wrap "merry widow" (Schuler); no wrap full-splice (Dufferin); Irish linen (Huebler); Irish linen (Schuler); Coated Irish linen (Meucci); Leather (Helmstetter); Leather (Helmstetter).

The Wrap

Some cues are designed without a wrap, but most cues feature a gripping area wrapped in nylon, Irish linen, leather, or cork. Irish linen is the de facto standard. The purpose of the wrap is to absorb hand perspiration and improve the player's purchase on the cue during play. Leather and cork are often available as an extra-cost option. As for what wrap is best, that is entirely a question of personal preference.

Kulungian: *A leather wrap is usually slightly thicker than a linen wrap and requires a deeper cut in the wood, so don't plan on switching from leather to linen after you buy the cue. The wrap is often overlooked in assessing the quality of a cue. Great cuemakers put on great wraps. Gus Szamboti was a master. Even if a Szamboti cue needs to be refin-*

Check the top of the wrap for ridges or depressions.

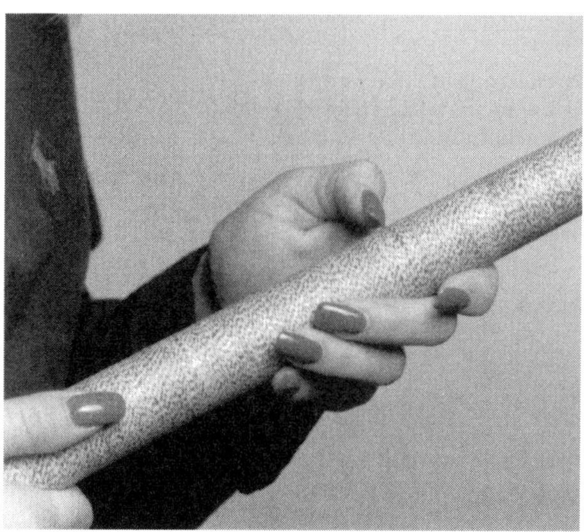

With an Irish linen or nylon wrap, check for tightness and evenness.

ished, the wrap should be preserved whenever possible. Unfortunately, the Cortland brand Irish linen that Szamboti and other cuemakers used to use is no longer commercially available.

Tests: With Irish linen or nylon, check the wrap for tightness and evenness. There should be no gaps or overlaps.

With leather and cork, check for evenness and smoothness. Leather wraps usually have a seam running the length of the wrap. The seam should be straight.

Run your finger over the

top and bottom of the wrap. There should be no ridges or depressions.

The Butt. Butt caps, top to bottom,: Multi-polymer plastic (Cousins); Delrin (Schuler); Delrin (Hercek); Exotic wood, ebony (Samsara); ivory substitute (Huebler). This photo also illustrates different afterwrap treatments.

The Butt Cap and Bumper

The *butt cap*, also called the butt plate, is essentially a ferrule at the end of the cue that protects the wood in the afterwrap from splitting and chipping. Butt cap materials include ivory, exotic woods, Delrin, phenolic, and a variety of other synthetics.

The butt cap is usually attached to the cue by both an adhesive bond and a mechanical connection, e.g., epoxy and a screw. Some butt caps are threaded and screw onto the cue. In addition to acting as a ferrule, the butt cap can serve the structural purpose of reinforcing or "locking down" the woods and decorative rings used in the butt sleeve.

Like the butt cap, the *bumper* protects the cue from shocks and damage when it is stood on end, e.g., between shots. Bumpers are made of rubber and are usually screwed into the butt cap, though other attaching techniques are used. Bumpers are especially important for cues with ivory or exotic wood butt caps, as these materials tend to be less durable and more expensive to repair or replace than synthetic butt caps.

Inlays

Inlays and decorative rings of ivory, mother-of-pearl, abalone, malachite, turquoise, exotic woods, precious metals, gem stones, and a wide variety of other materials are used to enhance the appearance of cues. Inlays may be executed by hand or with pantograph or CNC equipment. Machine-cut inlays usually have slightly rounded points, reflecting the radius of the cutting tool used to cut the inlay pocket and piece. Sharp points usually indicate that the inlays were done by hand or that the cuemaker worked the inlays by hand after executing the initial cuts by machine.

Inlays are for decorative purposes only. A custom cuemaker's $6,000 heavily-inlaid cue should not be expected to play any better than his plain-Jane $600 cue. With higher-priced cues, one is paying for high-quality materials – woods, hardware, adhesives, inlays, finish – and for the time and skill the cuemaker puts into creating and executing the aesthetic design.

Kulungian: *Some people say that a lot of inlays detract from a cue's performance. I've played with some super-fancy, heavily-inlayed cues that played great. I've played with some very plain cues, not an inlay in them, that played terribly.*

Test: Examine the inlays. Are they cleanly executed? Does each inlay fit tightly in its pocket, or is wood filler visible around it? Are any inlays sunk too deeply and covered with an excess of finish?

Roll the cue in your hand to check for raised inlays.

Roll the cue in your hand. Have the inlays lifted up through the finish? (Rolling the cue in your hand in a piece of paper will exaggerate any ridges or raised inlays, but some cuemakers feel that this is too severe an criterion of quality assessment.)

The Finish

Some type of finish is usually applied to the butt of the cue and to the first several inches of the shaft past the joint. The purpose of the finish is to protect the cue against dings and dents, and to inhibit the moisture transfers that occur with changes in relative humidity. The finish can also add luster and beauty to the cue.

Many finishing methods have been used on pool cues over the years: lacquer, shellac, oil, water conversion, and others. These traditional finishing methods had some disadvantages, including: fading in sunlight (UV radiation); cracking with temperature changes; and deteriorating through contact with perspiration.

Some modern cuemakers still use traditional finishing methods. Oil finishes offer a rich, low-gloss or matte look. Depending on the type of oil and techniques used, a shiny finish can also be achieved. An oil finish must be reapplied from time to time, and so requires more upkeep than other finishes. Oil finishes can be problematic in terms of repairs because 1) the oil tends to darken the wood, making color matching difficult; and 2) the oil penetrates the wood, making it difficult for adhesives to bond.

Compared to traditional methods, modern finishes are considered to be more durable, i.e., resistant to chipping, denting, and fading in sunlight. They are clear, hard, and can be buffed to a very high gloss. The modern finishes of choice are two and three-part catalyzed urethanes, acrylics, and UV-curable polymers. Most custom cuemakers use a urethane finish, which is essentially an automotive clear-coat finish.

Most finishing procedures are very time consuming. A coat of finish is applied, allowed to dry, sanded, then another coat is applied. This process is repeated until a suitable thickness has been achieved, usually about five mils (a mil is a thousandth of an inch; a human hair is about three mils thick).

Urethane finishes require about 30 days to cure to final hardness. (A new cue with a urethane finish, like a new car, should not be waxed for 30 days. Waxing prevents the clear coat finish from curing properly.) Unlike urethane finishes, UV-curable polymer finishes cure very quickly. They are also very hard and clear. The equipment required to produce this finish is quite expensive, however – up to $20,000 for a simple system – which may explain why UV-cured finishes are offered primarily by large manufacturers like McDermott and Viking.

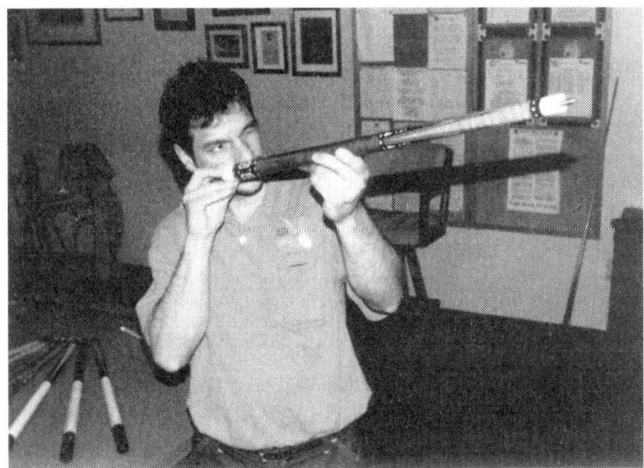

Sight down the cue to look for flat spots or flaws in the finish.

Kulungian: *You want a finish that's clear as opposed to cloudy so when you look through the finish you can see the colors and the veneers and the grain of the wood. The finish is there to protect the wood, not obscure it!*

Tests: Examine the finish for clarity and luster.

Hold the butt up to your cheek and sight down it toward a light source. Then slowly rotate the cue as you tilt it slightly up and down. This will allow you to spot any flaws or flat spots in the finish. (You can use the same procedure to spot flaws in the shaft.)

Measurements -- Length & Weight

The standard length of the modern two-piece cue is 58 inches, though custom lengths are available from most cuemakers and manufacturers. Weights range from 18 to 21 ounces. Most players opt for a cue between 19 and 20 ounces, though lighter cues seem to be gaining in popularity.

Pool cues used to be shorter and heavier, 57 inches and 19 to 22 ounces. Some experts suggest that longer cues are a response to an increase in average height. That may be so, but improvements in equipment over the years have played an important role. Tables are smaller (9 feet versus 10 feet), cloth is faster, and phenolic resin balls are more lively than the ivory or composite clay balls they replaced. Consequently, a lighter, less rigid (i.e., longer) cue is able to move the balls around the table. Another factor in longer cues may be the growing tendency for players to shoot from a very low position over the cue.

In his book *The Science of Pocket Billiards*, Jack Koehler states that the kinetic energy created by the movement of the cue and applied to the cue ball is a function of: 1) the weight of the cue and 2) the velocity of the cue when it strikes the cue ball. According to this formula, a heavier cue does not need to move as fast as a lighter cue to exert the same amount of energy on the cue ball. Although the differences will be minor, from this formula Koehler concludes that a lighter cue will offer superior cue ball speed control, because more of the energy created by the stroke is due to speed. A heavier cue will offer superior accuracy, because directional control is easier to maintain with the slower stroke.

Kulungian: *I encourage people to stay between 19 and 20 ounces. Newer players usually do better with a slightly heavier cue. The extra weight helps with accuracy and putting action on the cue ball. As a player's game and stroke develop, and speed control becomes more important, there is a tendency to switch to a slightly lighter cue.*

Tests: The weight marked on a cue may not be accurate. Use a mail scale to weigh the cue if exactitude is important to you.

Note: The weight of a cue varies slightly with changes in climate. A cue will tend to weigh more during humid seasons and less during dry seasons. A cue may also lose or gain weight if moved to a drier or more humid climate.

Balance

Balance is determined by how a cue's weight is distributed. The balance point is the point that evenly divides the cue's weight, like the fulcrum of a level teeter totter. Many suggest that a well-balanced cue will feel lighter in the player's hands than its actual weight.

Some cuemakers and manufacturers weight their cues with metal bolts in the butt sleeve, which can result in a butt-heavy cue unless that weight is compensated elsewhere in the cue. Other cuemakers avoid butt-heaviness by placing their weight bolts farther up in the cue, under the wrap. Still other cuemakers add no metal at all, achieving the weight and balance they want by selecting lighter or heavier pieces and types of wood during construction. This approach allows the weight of the cue to be more evenly distributed along its length, which, according to its proponents, improves the cue's balance and feel.

To determine the balance point, hold the cue horizontally between your thumb and index finger.

The common practice is to define the balance point of cues by measuring from the butt cap or the top of the wrap, e.g.,

18 inches from the butt, two inches above the wrap. Unfortunately, neither of these measurements is entirely reliable for comparative purposes, as both cue length and wrap placement can vary from cue to cue. It may be more practical to measure the balance point from the tip.

Kulungian: *Cuemakers and cue manufacturers have different philosophies, but most balance points are between 17 and 20 inches from the butt or one to two inches above the wrap, which translates into 38 to 41 inches from the tip of a 58 inch cue.*

The balance point that's right for you depends on how you play and what you're most comfortable with. If you use an open bridge, however, you probably want a more forward-balanced cue, to avoid a tendency for the tip of the cue to rise when you're shooting.

Test: Hold the cue horizontally between your thumb and index finger slightly above the wrap. Then move the cue forward or back until it balances, resting level. That is the cue's balance point.

A more precise method of determining the balance point of a cue is to use a common six-sided pencil as a fulcrum. Lay the pencil on the bed of a pool table and balance the cue across it.

In Closing

A pool cue is a tool for pocketing balls. The cue buyer's task is to find a cue that is a good match for his or her style of play. A broad selection of high-quality cues is available across a wide price range. Find a reputable cue dealer. Try a variety of cues. Look for build quality, hit, and playability before you look for looks. Expect to pay at least $75. The more you know when you start shopping, the better your chances will be of finding a cue that's right for you, at the right price. It is hoped that this pool cue primer has helped to get you off to a good start.

It is important to remember that, while the criteria of build quality are well-established, "the truth" about cue performance is still far from clear, so keep an open mind. It's also a good idea to regard with a degree of skepticism what you hear down at the pool hall and what you read in advertisements, magazine articles, and books (including this one) about what makes a cue "good-hitting" or "good-playing." A good-playing cue is one that brings out the best in your game. Perhaps that's why the best-playing cues always seem to find their way into the hands of the best players!

Bibliography

Byrne, Robert.
Byrne's Standard Book of Pool and Billiards.
San Diego: Harcourt Brace Jovanovich, 1987.

Jewett, Bob.
"Squirt Testing."
Billiards Digest,
August 1994, pp. 34-38.

Koehler, Jack.
The Science of Pocket Billiards.
Laguna Hills: Sportology Publications, 1989.

Schuler, Ray.
"The Strait Schtick."
The National Billiard News, November, 1983; December, 1983; September, 1994; May 1984.

Shamos, Mike.
The Illustrated Encyclopedia of Billiards.
New York: Lyons & Burford, 1993.

Simpson, Brad.
Blue Book of Pool Cues.
Minneapolis: Blue Book Publications, 1996

Stein, Victor and Paul Rubino.
The Billiard Encyclopedia.
New York: The Billiard Encyclopedia, 1994.

U.S. Department of Agriculture.
Wood Handbook.
Washington, D.C.: U.S. Government Printing Office, 1955.

Directory of Cue Makers

A.M.F. Legacy Cues
106 Lyford St.
Bland, MO 65014
800-646-3557

Adam Custom Cues
25 Hutcheson Pl.
Lynbrook, NY 11563
800-645-2162

AE Cues
3429 S. Ouray Way
Aurora, CO 80013
303-766-8301

Allen's Custom Cues
14810 Kornblum Ave.
Hawthorne, CA 90250-8437
310-675-4005

Bender Cues
HC60 Box 3890
Delta Junction, AK 99737
907-895-4725

Benson Cue
P.O. Box 6563
Kennewick WA 99336
509-586-7277

Bill Schick Originals
8101 Kingston Rd. Suite 112
Shreveport, LA 71106
318-688-8070

Bill McDaniel Cues
586 Airway Blvd.
Jackson, TN 38301
901-424-4455

Black Boar Industries
5110 College Ave.
College Park, MD 20740
301-277-3236

Bludworth Custom Cues
Rt. 1 Box 1542
Quitman, TX 75783
903-967-3360

Bob Hunter Custom Cues
P.O. Box 21866
Carson City, NV 89721
702-884-CUES

Bob Runde Cues
21751 65th St.
Bristol, WI 53104
414-857-6533

Bourque Custom Made Cues
4012 Venice Rd. Lot 100
Sandusky, OH 44870
419-626-9723

Brunswick Billiards
8663 196th Ave.
Bristol, WI 53014-0068
414-857-7489

Capone Cues
38 Wilson Ave.
Mercerville, NJ 08619
609-586-8165

Chilton Custom Cues
135 11th. Ave South
South St. Paul, MN 55075
612-457-0527

Clawson Cues
5055-5 St. Augustine Rd.
Jacksonville, FL 32207
904-448-8748

Cognoscenti Cues
3711 N. Ravenswood
Chicago, IL 60613
773-348-7154

Corsair Custom Cues
19841 Cloucester Lane
Huntington Beach, CA 92646
714-968-8566

Cousins Custom Cues
W-3 Winona Park Dr.
Bernhards Bay, NY 13028
315-675-8112

Creative Inventions
7745 Alabama St. Unit#1
Canoga Park, CA 91304
818-883-5131

Cue Master
2422 E. 37th Ave.
Spokane, WA 99223
509-448-2226

Custom Cues
201 Ranger Rd.
Wisconsin Rapids, WI 54494
715-325-3696

Dale Patten Cues
411 Emerald
Redondo Beach, CA 90277
310-372-0479

Danny Tibbetts Cues
112 Golden Hill Dr.
Woodstock, GA 30189
770-926-0475

David Tice Custom Cues
16441 Lakeview Dr.
Leavenworth, WA 98826
509-763-3020

Dennis Deickman Custom Cues
P.O. Box 369
Manchester, MI 48158
313-428-1161

Dishaw Custom Cues
2608 Bellevue Ave.
Syracuse, NY 13219
315-472-4712

Don Doyon Custom Cues
733 Riverside Dr.
Augusta, ME 04330
207-623-3589

DP Custom Cues
2175 Kingsley Ave. Suite 201
Orange Park, FL 32073
904-276-4213

Dufferin, Inc.
4240 Grove Ave.
Gurnee, IL 60031
847-244-4762

Ed Young Custom Cues
429 West Ohio St. Unit 117
Chicago, IL 60610
312-519-2505

Edgenet Inc.
8511 Wellsford Place Suite#A.
Santa Fe Springs, CA 90670
310-464-1660

Elite Custom Cues
P.O. Box 4224
Lincoln, NE 68504-0224
402-486-4407

Embassy Cue Co.
56 Crescent Blvd.
Gloucester City, NJ 08030
609-742-7666

Ernie Martinez Custom Cues
6035 East 76th Ave. Unit#G
Commerce City, CO 80022
303-289-3209

Espiritu Custom Cues
6162 Hwy. 18
Brandon, MS 39042
601-825-7077

Falcon Cue Co.
56 Crescant Blvd.
Gloucester City, NJ 08030
609-742-7666

Frank Fisher Custom Cues
429 W. Maple St.
Johnson City, TN 37604
800-481-6732

GB Custom Cues
15506 St. Cloud Dr.
Houston, TX 77062
713-480-2893

GCue
2255 Computer Ave.
Willow Grove, PA 19090
800-423-3220

Gem Cues
P.O. Box 6364
Lake Charles, LA 70606

Gilbert Custom Cues
827 Frazier Rd.
Clever, MO 65631
417-743-2759

Ginucue
5424 Vineland Ave.
North Hollywood, CA 91601
818-509-0454

Hadrianus Cue Co.
3701 South 60th Court
Cicero, IL 60804
708-652-5952

Hagan Cue
331 N Corinne Dr.
Gilbert, AZ 85234
602-926-7422

Hal Hawkins Cues
W3940 Box 50, Mitchell
Eau Claire, WI 54701
715-836-9196

Harold Morey Cues
2703 King Settlement
Alpena, MI 49707
517-379-3683

Hercek Custom Cues
1352 Armour Blvd.
Mundelein, IL 60060
847-680-7498

Hicks Sticks
Rt. 1 Box 175
Stronghurst, IL 61480
309-924-1127

Howard Cues
1202 W. Green Valley
Bensenville, IL 60106
708-595-0037

Huebler Industries
600 Jefferson St.
Linn, MO 65051
314-897-3692

Hunter Classics Custom Cues
172 La Luz Gate Rd.
Alamagordo, NM 88310
505-437-1972

Hurricane Cue Co.
808 Coleman Blvd.
Mt. Pleasant, SC 29464
803-881-6187

It's George
403 Lake St.
Shreveport, LA 71101
800-343-6743

J&J America
5815 Guatemala Way
Buena Park, CA 90620
714-994-5928

J. Pechauer Custom Cues
4140 Veld Ave.
Green Bay, WI 54313
414-434-7755

J.B. Custom Cues
1020 Newman Lane
Lexington, KY 40515
606-271-4140

Jackson Cue Co.
465 N. Main St.
West Bend, WI 53095
414-334-0616

Jensen Custom Cues
9135 Cuyhanga Dr.
Baton Rouge, LA 70815
504-924-4517

Jerico Cues
34 Field
Clyde, TX 79510
800-971-3142

Jim Buss Customer Cues
15506 St. Cloud Dr.
Houston, TX 77062
713-480-2893

John Guffey Customer Cues
2422 Cedar Oak
Edmond, OK 73013
405-359-2047

Josey Custom Cues
12 Wymberly Way
Savannah, GA 31406
912-356-1816

Joss Cues Ltd.
8749 Mylander Ln.
Towson, MD 21204
410-821-0064

Josswest
1310 Ranch Rd. 620 South
Austin, TX 78734
512-263-3452

J-S Sales Company Inc.
5 South Fulton Ave
Mt. Vernon, NY 10550
800-431-2944

Judd's Custom Cues
552 Highlander
Riverside, CA 92507
909-782-8010

Karella Corp.
25 Hutcheson
Lynbrook, NY 11563
516-593-5050

Kelly Cues
2615 Ryan Dr.
Indianapolis, IN 46220
317-251-0684

Kikel Custom Cues
1614 b N. Academy Blvd.
Colorado Springs, CO 80909
719-596-7349

Lambros Cues
5603A Pulaski Hwy.
Baltimore, MD 21205
410-325-6141

Mace Custom Cues
By Rick Howard
8246 Verano
Navarre, FL 32566
904-939-1454

Mali Co.
257 Park Ave. S.
New York, NY 10010
212-475-4960

Mariposa Cue Co.
5935 Irving Park Rd.
Chicago, IL 60634
708-585-1270

Maximum Cue
7472 Old Hwy. 78
Olive Branch, MS 38654
601-893-2155

McDermott Cue Mfg. Inc.
W146 N9560 Held Dr.
Menomonee Falls, WI 53051
414-251-4090

McWorter Custom Cues
82 S. Anacapa St.
Ventura, CA 93001
805-648-2225

Meucci Originals Inc.
7472 Old Hwy. 78
Olive Branch, MS 38654
601-895-4877

Michael Morgan Cues
216 N. Chestnut St.
North Massapequa, NY 11758
516-799-8203

Michael's Custom Cues
1729 St. Claire
Racine, WI 53402
414-633-7657

Mid West Custom Cues
720 1st. Ave. So.
South St. Paul, MN 55075
612-455-3435

Mohawk Cue Co.
56 Crescant Blvd.
Gloucester City, NJ 08030
609-742-7666

Mottey Custom Cues
2844 Broadway Ave.
Pittsburg, PA 15216
412-881-9211

Mr. Billiard Custom Cues
35 Administration Rd.
Concord, Ontario L4K 3G9
800-661-0106

Mueller Sporting Goods
4825 S. 16th St.
Lincoln, NE 68512
800-627-8888

Northern Cues
P.O. Box 153
Norway MI 49870
906-563-5188

Nova Cues, Inc.
2100 Northwestern Ave.
West Bend, WI 53095
414-335-2600

Oliver Stops Original
P.O. Box 781
Alpharetta, GA 30201
888-9-OLIVER

OMEGA/dpk Cue Company
950 N. Rand Rd.
Wauconda, IL 60084
847-526-4411

ORCHID, U.S.A. Custom Cues
25 Hutcheson Pl.
Lynbrook, NJ 11563
800-645-2162

Padgett Custom Cues
P.O. Box 1145
Duarte, CA 91010-1145
818-359-CUES

Parrot Cue
2125 Staples Mill Rd.
Richmond, VA 23230
804-358-7665

Patrick Custom Cues
3304 Terrace Lane
Granite City, IL 62040
618-877-7144

Pete Campbell Cues
56 Sheldon Rd.
Wrentham, MA 02093
508-384-2260

pfd Custom Cues
213 Flood Rd.
Marlborough, CT 06447
860-295-8500

Phillippi Custom Cues
182 11th St.
Pasadena, MD 21122
410-437-2386

Picone Cues
630 SW Davie Blvd.
Fort Lauderdale, FL 33315
305-767-9004

Players Cues
2899 Powers Ave. Unit#1
Jacksonville, FL 32207
800-232-3654

Porcupine Cues
P.O. Box 588
Meridianville, AL 35759
800-232-3654

The Powell Agency
8866 Oak Circle
Tampa, FL 33615

Prather Cue
200 S. Main
Mooreland, OK 73852
405-994-2414

Privilege Fine Billiard Cues
P.O. Box 955
Leakey, TX 78873
713-852-5025

Ravenzahn Cues
1608 Pennsylvania Ave. E.
Warren, PA 16365
814-723-8322

Rhino Cues
1414 Ave. C.
Danbury, TX 77534
409-922-8670

Richard Black
Custom Crafted Cues
P.O. Box 1886
Humble, TX 77347
713-852-5025

Richard Chudy Custom Cues
1867 Lucille Ln.
Pleasant Hill, CA 94523
510-798-4369

Rikard Custom Cues
1008 12th St.
Galena Park, TX 77547
713-450-1275

Robinson Custom Cues
13634 N. 51st. Way
Scottsdale, AZ 85254
602-996-5022

Rubino Cues
110 Lynden Ave.
New Windsor, NY 12553
914-496-3795

Sailor Cues
1649 Taylor Avenue
Racine, WI 53403

Samsara Cues
800 W. Hollis St.
Nashua, NH 03062
603-883-7686

Schmelke Mfg. Inc.
1879 28th Ave.
Rice Lake, WI 54868
715-234-6553

Schon Cues
3812 W. Burnham
Milwaukee, WI 53221
414-383-9661

Schrager Cues
7255 Atoll Ave.
North Hollywood, CA 91605
818-764-0187

Schuler Cue
540 West Colfax Street #2
Palatine, IL 60067
888-THE-1CUE
847-776-7769
Fax 847-776-6826

Shaman Cues
205 Horseshoe Circle
Las Cruces, NM 88005
505-524-0392

Sherm Cues
P.O. Box 54698
Cincinnati, OH 45254-0698
513-231-8507

Sigel's World Class Cues, Inc.
3401 Lake Breeze Dr.
Orlando, FL 32808
407-521-POOL

Silver Fox
3233 Sunset Way
Bellingham, WA 98226
360-758-7304

South West Cues
4608 Nolan Ln.
Las Vegas, NV 89107
702-870-9615

Star Cue Co.
428 Jefferson
Miami, FL 33139
305-673-1133

Stealth Cue
700 Industrial Dr.
Cary, IL 60013
847-516-4700

Stonier's Cues
2375 Fruitridge Rd.
Sacramento, CA 95822
916-456-2284

Stout Cue Mfg.
692 Back Creek Rd.
Asheboro, NC 27203

Syra Cues by RK
105 Hillside Way
Camillas, NY 13031
315-488-6621

Szamboti Cues Inc.
1914 Midfield Rd.
Feasterville, PA 19053
215-357-5032

Tad's Custom Cue
8300 Cerritos Ave.
Stanton, CA 90680

Thomas Wayne Cues
3605 Arctic Blvd. #1806
Anchorage, AK 99503
907-349-3743

Tim Scruggs Custom Cues, Inc.
900 Leeds Ave.
Baltimore, MD 21229
410-247-1231

Tom Harris Cues
P.O. Box 120036
East Haven, CT 06512
203-483-5777

Thunder Cue Co.
810 W. 56 Hwy.
Olathe, KS 66061
913-780-5740

Val Hall Cues
3611 Ellwood
Berkley, MI 48072
810-546-4403

Verl Horn Cues
Box 880
Mooreland, OK 73852
405-994-5970

Viking Cue Mfg. Inc.
2710 Syene Rd.
Madison, WI 53713
608-271-5155

Weston Custom Cues
266 Cobb Ln.
Hot Springs, AR 71901
501-624-7164

Woodworth Cues
4974 Greyhawk
San Antonio, TX 78217
210-656-6479

Zar Cues
5482 Sherwood
Jackson, MI 49201
517-750-4710

About The Author

Stephen Mayhew's writing career includes stints as a translator of screenplays in Paris, France, as a business writer in San Francisco, CA, and as a director of business communications in Hartford, CT. He is best known in pool circles for his series of in-depth cuemaker interviews published in *All About Pool.* A collection of these interviews is slated for publication by Merrimack Publishing, Inc. under the title, *Cuemaking in Theory and Practice.* Mr. Mayhew currently works as a free-lance writer in Bowling Green, OH.